Mikey & Me

A journey of faith through autism

by
Amitha Esther Vanaguntla

"The author of this book is my niece, and I knew this family from their childhood.

I appreciate seeing the faith, efforts and skills of Esther, Rao and Isaac as they work through a persistent agony with their son Michael's autism, turning it into praise and honour to the Living God. It was completely perplexing in the early stages with Michael, and God led them to the appropriate institutions in NZ. They have diagnosed the situation and found the best course of action. Though it is a complicated situation for Mikey, they totally depend in faith on the Living God and He has provided them with enough strength to treat him in a prayerful way. Esther mentions the purpose of migrating to NZ, to adore the Almighty God in all situations, as things could have been difficult in India. The demonstration of their faith in God made them calm in their ceaseless challenges with autism. Esther points out that people do not understand Mikey's situation and stare at him instead of assisting. These emerging frustrations became common and thereafter they learned not to worry what society thinks. This book reveals that parental behaviour and comprehension of a child's circumstances are the most essential factors to manage the state of the child.

This family stands as an example to society that any given circumstance can be confronted, without panic, with faith in God. This book can be a blessing for those facing the same type of situation. They can be encouraged without losing hope, and this book may be utilised as their guide. I pray Almighty God that Michael can be a useful gentleman to a needful society. God bless you."

— C. Vijayaseker Abraham

"We read Mikey and Me: A Journey of Faith through Autism, written by my sister. It's a really heart-touching personal experience and journey, going through this new thing in our family (Autism). We felt so sad when we came to know about Mikey's situation in his very early days, every one of us prayed for my sister's family and still pray continuously to God for His mighty grace, strength and mercy. In this book when you go through each chapter you can feel the pain, but at the same time peace and calmness through Jesus Christ's presence in each and every second of our life. Let's hope everyone reads and appreciates our journey through faith and hope tackling autism. May God bless Mikey abundantly and be with him."
— Aaron Chinnamallela (Brother) and Prashanthi (Sister-in-Law)

"For those who have never heard of nor understand Autism, this easy-to-read personal journey will tug at your emotions; open your eyes and ears to the struggles that families looking after children with disabilities may face; and at the same time it challenges those who profess Christ as their Lord to stay faithful through life's challenges."
— Dr Edwin Yip

"It was very well written and elaborated with real life experiences and events that happened in Esther's life. It was an awe-inspiring book narrated in excellent manner."
— Aruna Kambhampati

"Esther's Christian faith shines through in this story of love as she and her family come to terms with finding out that their beloved youngest son and brother, Mikey, has a diagnosis of autism.

Esther and I have worked closely together as part of the team at BBCK. For the more than 13 years we have worked together, I have seen Esther's capabilities expand. Her compassion and understanding of the needs of young children has deepened, especially for those with special needs. She brings joy wherever she goes; her wonderful sense of humour is always close to the surface. All of this has made her a great blessing and my life is enriched through knowing her."
— Nancy O'Connor

Amitha Esther Vanaguntla
Email: estheramitha@gmail.com

Unless indicated otherwise, Scripture quotations taken from New International Version (NIV) Holy Bible, New International Version®, NIV® Copyright ©1973, 1978, 1984, 2011 by Biblica, Inc.® Used by permission. All rights reserved worldwide.

Written and published by:
Amitha Esther Vanaguntla

Foreword by: Rev. Andrew Marshall, Senior Pastor, Blockhouse Bay Community Church, National Director of Alliance Churches of New Zealand
Project management:
Wild Side Publishing
www.wildsidepublishing.com
Cover design and text layout:
Wild Side Design
www.wildsidedesign.net

Cataloguing in Publication Data:
Title: Mikey and Me: A Journey of Faith through Autism
ISBN: 978-0-473-42490-9 (pbk.)
Subjects: Memoir, Biography, Christian Living, Autism, Mental Health, Language Therapy

International listing 2018 Ingram Spark

CONTENTS

This book is dedicated to the Almighty God, my husband Rao
and my son Isaac, who shared this journey with me.

FOREWORD

I was surprised and honoured to be asked to write the foreword for this wonderful book. The Vanaguntla family have been part of our church whanau since 2002 and are a very precious family to us, and to me personally. They are what I describe as "quiet achievers", a deeply respected quality in New Zealand ascribed to people who achieve a great deal without drawing unnecessary attention to themselves.

This book is an example of this humble quality at work. Esther has written a wonderful account of her family's journey with the challenges of Mikey's autism. Their strong Christian faith weaves its way through the book which is laced with helpful information about autism and an honest account of the struggles experienced, the joy in the achievements made, and the hope of a God who is always there with them.

The book has a wealth of practical information and advice for people who are dealing with autism in their own families, as well as those of us who simply want to understand how to support families more closely impacted by this condition. The length of the book, the quality of the people in the heart of the story, and the style of writing make it an irresistible read that will be a source of hope and blessing to people all over the world.

Rev. Andrew Marshall
Senior Pastor, Blockhouse Bay Community Church
National Director, Alliance Churches of New Zealand

INTRODUCTION

I was born and brought up in an environment where I was taught to depend on God for everything. I could talk to Him as a friend or a family member. This book is the story of how God helped me through many twists and turns. He was beside me and sometimes even carried me in His arms.

I migrated to New Zealand with my husband and my two year old son Isaac in 2002. My second son Michael was born at the end of that year. Michael is the reason for writing this book. At two and a half years old, Michael was diagnosed with autism. This brought a tremendous, unforeseen change into our lives.

I hope this book, drawn out of my personal experiences, will help you to understand the effects of Autism. I hope this book helps you as you take that step of faith towards God.

First, I would like to thank God for everything He has done in my life. Secondly, I want to thank my husband and my son Isaac, my mother for encouraging me through her prayers, and my siblings and their families for encouraging me to write this book.

I would like to thank Paromita for helping me in the process of editing, Ben for proofreading, Andrew for the Foreword, and Janet Curle for designing the cover. I also want to thank each person who has read my book and shared their thoughts.

Heart-felt thanks to the speech language therapists, occupational therapists, class teachers, social workers, teacher aides, caregivers and all the other professionals and specialists who have been working with Mikey.

ISAAC: ABOUT MIKEY

Although Mikey may get a lot more attention and more leniency at home, it's understandable to me. I do sometimes feel like I'm being left out but that's bound to happen so I try not to think about it too much, because my responsibility is to take care of him, not be jealous of him.

I see Mikey as a challenge that God gave us, especially me. If we can take care of this gift from God and show him the right path to go, that would make God especially happy.

I'm usually the only one that can connect to Mikey about things that are involved in his life, because I've already been in contact with them when I was younger and because I can relate to his age, being just a few years older than him. It makes me glad that he can talk to me about things happening in school, because sometimes parents can be a little oblivious to what's really going on.

I also try to be fair but firm on him, which can sometimes have a negative effect on him, but he also needs to learn that not everything will be handed to him on a silver platter. I try to make him a bit more independent, rather than doing things for him so that he can learn to start doing things for himself now, instead of later when it proves more difficult.

Chapter 1

I come from a long line of Christian believers. My parents had four children – two daughters and two sons. I learned valuable lessons about faith from my parents. My father was very humble, and whatever work was given to him, he did it with passion. My mother was very praycrful and was always on her knees praying for each and every member of the family and their needs.

As a family, we always sought God's guidance before we began anything. When we had problems, my mum used to discuss them with us and we prayed together. I believe that God always hears our prayers and answers them in His own time. Prayer was a very important part of my life. I learnt to pray at a young age. My mother also taught me to thank God for listening to and answering our prayers. "Give thanks to the Lord, for He is good; His love endures forever". I thank her for teaching me to always pray — whether I have had trials and tribulations, or a perfect day. I may not have the time to kneel down and pray but I always talk to God wherever I am.

After my graduation, my father encouraged me to do a postgraduate degree in Economics. I did that, then I completed a teacher training course at a Christian college called St Alphonsa's College of Education, in Hyderabad. While I was in training, our English lecturer told us she was going to leave the job because she was moving to New Zealand. That was the first time I heard about New Zealand. Little did I know that someday the Lord would bring me to this country. The day after I finished my training I got my first job as a lecturer in Economics. God taught me that whatever situation I go through, He is with me holding my hand. If there is a need, He will carry me. His angels are watching over me. I can talk to God at any time and any place.

While I was working as a lecturer I married Rao, in August 1998. Rao was also brought up in a Christian family. I knew him from my childhood. We went to Sunday school and church together. Rao was then an Assistant Professor at Osmania University.

After a year, in October 1999, we were blessed with a baby boy. We named him Isaac, which means 'laughter'. He weighed 3.5kg and was a healthy baby.

Chapter 2

One day, out of the blue, my uncle (Dad's brother) suggested that we go to New Zealand. He always wanted to live in New Zealand but, for some reason, his application was rejected. Some of his friends were living in the country and he was keen to send me and Rao. In fact, he even consulted an agent and started the application process. We applied for Permanent Residency. I prayed, 'God, if it is your will, will you send us.' By God's grace, our application was successful and six months later we were granted Permanent Residency.

We packed our bags and said our goodbyes to our family and friends. It was sad to leave home. We reached Auckland on 3 February, 2002.

It was a new country for us and new challenges lay ahead. We reached a point where we found that whatever money we brought with us was spent on rent, food and other necessaries. Each week we had only a few dollars to spend, which was enough for us to survive. The only weapon I had was prayer. Rao and I started to pray for our jobs and needs. We believed that God had a plan and purpose for bringing us to this new land. We believed that God would look after our needs. He was not going to leave or forsake us.

As Hebrews 13:5 says,

"I will never leave you nor forsake you."

A month later, I found out that I was pregnant. It was tough with the morning sickness. I was also worried about how we would survive since we had no work. But God reminded me again that I don't need to worry about anything. As Philippians 4:6 says,

"Do not be anxious about anything, but in everything by prayer and supplication with thanksgiving let your requests be made known to God."

Though there were some hiccups in the beginning, God helped me and my family to settle down in the new country.

Our main goal was to find work. Though I was pregnant, I continued to look for a job. I attended two interviews — one at a daycare and another at a petrol station. I was rejected for both jobs as I had higher qualifications. Physically, it was a difficult time, too. I was unable to eat well and sometimes I would throw up everything I ate. I didn't go to the doctor. The truth is, we were both struggling to find jobs, and Isaac was still little, and I was afraid of having my second child in this situation.

But our Father answered our prayers and my husband got a job in a vegetable and fruit export company. I was alone with Isaac at home. I didn't know anyone and stayed home all day. God helped me throughout my pregnancy.

Chapter 3

It was amazing how God brought things together. Michael was born in November 2002. There were no complications and he was a healthy 2.9kg baby. Rao had a good job at Sky City while I was looking after Michael (Mikey) at home. Isaac was 3 and we enrolled him in a kindergarten near our home. Mikey was a beautiful boy who progressed well. When he was 3 months old, he was responsive and was putting his hands in his mouth. He held his head well and even rolled over. I was getting frustrated as I was staying home and wanted to work.

When Mikey was 6 months old, I joined a computer training programme at Unitec. Rao dropped Isaac and Mikey at a home-based daycare and picked them up in the evening. While I was at Unitec, my teachers recommended that I enrol for the teacher training programme. The following year, I applied for Early Childhood Education (ECE) training and was accepted.

As a part of my training, I had to do work experience at an ECE centre for 15 hours a week. I approached Andrew Marshall, our church pastor, and he introduced me to Antonia, the Director of Blockhouse Bay Christian Kindergarten (BBCK), which was connected to the Blockhouse Bay Community Church (BBCC). I started working there as a volunteer.

I didn't know how to drive so Rao dropped me at the kindergarten every day. Isaac was enrolled at the Kindergarten and Mikey was still going to the daycare. Our lives were busy. Rao was finding it very hard to work in the mornings so he opted to work night shifts. It was getting more and more stressful for me to manage everything.

Mikey was growing well, and he was called Mr Smiley at church. At 9 months, he said, "Mum" and "Dad" in Telugu. He started eating meat, veggies and Kari Care. At 15 months, he was walking, running and stopping to pick things up, and eating a similar diet to us. He understood simple requests like bringing the remote. He had good eye/hand coordination. At one and a half, he knew his numbers (from 1 to 10).

When he turned 2, he was very active, ate a variety of foods, and developed well, although his speech was delayed. The Plunket nurse (Plunket is New Zealand's largest provider of support services for the development, health and wellbeing of children under 5) suggested we speak only one language with him. Since we spoke Telugu and English at home and sometimes watched Hindi programmes on TV, she suggested that Mikey was probably confused. She also asked us to use some specific strategies – for instance, we had to face him when talking to him, talk to him frequently, read stories, discuss TV with him, sing songs, and take him to playgroup to play with other children. The Plunket nurse referred us to Group Special Education (GSE) in 2005. GSE is the Ministry of Education department that works with children with special needs and their families.

As the days passed, we were very worried about Mikey's speech. We took him to our General Practitioner (GP) and she referred us to the National Audiology Centre for a hearing test. At 2 years and 7 months old, Mikey was then referred for a speech-language screening assessment. We had an appointment with the developmental paediatrician (DP). He recommended that Mikey receive comprehensive assessment from a speech language therapist (SLT) and an early intervention teacher (EIT). The DP provided some exercises to encourage Mikey's eye contact and vocalisation.

Chapter 4

We had enrolled Mikey at BBCK, where I was working as a volunteer. He was going to start kindergarten when he turned 3. One day, I learned that an SLT and a psychologist were visiting the kindergarten, and I got permission from the director to allow Mikey to see the specialists. They were in the staff room when I entered with Mikey. One of them started blowing bubbles and asked Mikey to pop them, but Mikey didn't respond to her or the bubbles. He was distracted and just wandered around in the room. We then had an appointment at the Early Intervention Service Clinic where I shared my concerns about Mikey's delayed language skills. After listening to me, the doctor interacted with Mikey for some time.

When the SLT counted from 1 to 9 and then paused, Mikey said "ten". Other words that he said were "Bujji" (my nickname) and "Akka" (sister). Mikey used a gesture for his dad to put a toy on the table. He was able to make eye contact with the SLT.

Mikey followed routine instructions like "come with me, I will wash your face". It was difficult for me and my husband to get Mikey's attention when speaking to him. He enjoyed drawing, playing with toy cars and simple puzzles. He carried a toy car wherever he went. He learned a lot of things by observing others. He used to operate the DVD/VCR independently.

The SLT sent us a report and a copy to the kindergarten director since Mikey was enrolled there. We had an appointment with the DP at the clinic. Mikey was 2 years and 8 months old. The DP asked Rao and me some questions and interacted with Mikey. After a while, she asked us, "Do you know about autism"? I looked at Rao and paused for a minute. Then I replied, "Yes, I've heard the word autism, as I'm currently training as an ECE teacher." The DP then said that Mikey demonstrated some features of autism with regard to delayed speech and language development and significant restriction in social activities. My mind was blank as she was talking and I couldn't hear a single word she was saying. When I came back to my senses, I remembered Acts 2:25,

"I saw the Lord always before me. Because He is always at my right hand, I will not be shaken."

After listening to this shocking news there was no time to think and digest it. Rao and I looked at each other. We both looked at the DP who had given us this information. She gave us some material about autism and described how Mikey has particular fixations with cartoons, cars, and water. He often seemed in a world of his own and would happily spend hours playing independently. He reciprocally played with Isaac.

Isaac was 5 then, and mature for his age. He was very co-operative and understanding with Mikey. Isaac and Mikey spent more time together. Mikey was very comfortable with his brother and Isaac easily understood whatever Mikey was saying to him.

As Isaac was growing up, he understood Mikey's situation. We parents always tried to treat both children equally even though Mikey needed more attention. Rao as a father enjoyed interacting with both boys. He regularly played cricket and badminton with them.

The DP then referred Mikey for an audiology assessment, ongoing speech and language therapy & an EIT. He was also referred for blood-Chromosomes, Fragile X, thyroid function,and iron studies tests. We were also asked to apply for a childhood disability allowance. She also sent us information regarding Autism NZ Inc. We were asked to bring Mikey for a review with the DP in 6 months.

On our way, back home Rao and I didn't say a single word to each other. There were many things going on in our minds. I asked, "God, why me?" I imagined that I got a call from the DP saying, "It was a mistake. There's nothing wrong with Mikey. Mikey is normal like other children." Then I realised that it was just an illusion. I was on my knees, "God, please help me in my new journey which seems really scary."

Mikey's test results came. His full blood count, iron studies, and Fragile X test, as well as all the other test results, were normal. The DP sent a report saying that clinical examination was unremarkable. Mikey had normal neurological, cardiovascular and respiratory and abdominal examinations. He has no neurocutaneous stigmata, which is a term used for a group of neurologic disorders, a tricky word I had never heard before.

It was time for me to start my new research project on 'autism', Autism Spectrum Disorder, or ASD. I looked up 'autism' online and there was a lot of information. I was reading in a hurry and looking for an instant cure which I could use for Mikey, as I wanted to fix whatever Mikey had. I wanted to do it as soon as possible. I spent a long time on my research.

The day after we found out, I shared Mikey's news with my director and colleagues at work. She had also read the SLT's report. She suggested that we enrol Mikey at another day care. Mikey might face challenges or create problems at the kindergarten which might upset me as a teacher and as a parent. She said that he would be happy at another place where I would just be a parent. I understood the situation and enrolled Mikey at a daycare near my house.

I was scared to share the news about Mikey's diagnosis at the new day care. Would they accept him if they knew he was autistic? But I informed the teachers and they contacted Special Education. Mikey attended day care for five full days each week. As parents, we both worried about Mikey's lack of intelligible speech, his reduced social interactions and his very brief attention span.

Mikey was observed by an educational psychologist at the day care and at home, at different times and in different situations. She used a range of methods like observations and direct play sessions at daycare, discussions with the teaching team, discussions with us (his parents), and a questionnaire we filled out called "Ages and Stages" (Bricker,

1992). This questionnaire covered different areas of development like communication, gross and fine motor skills, problem-solving skills, person-social and over-all growth and development.

As I grappled with these challenges, God gradually revealed to me that He created Mikey in his own image and placed him in our family. He knows that Mikey was born with special needs. As Jeremiah 1:5 says,

"Before I formed you in the womb I knew you, and before you were born I consecrated you."

This Bible verse has assured me that God chose our family for Mikey. Once I realised God's wonderful and amazing works, I started praising Him for giving Mikey as a precious gift to us. I decided there was no turning back, no tears and no sorrow.

Chapter 5

It was a weekend and I was cleaning the house in the afternoon. Suddenly I felt dizzy and I stopped what I was doing. I tried to walk to the nearest sofa but couldn't, I was falling. I quickly grabbed some support and with great difficulty managed to reach the couch. Following this, I regularly started getting dizzy spells. They became a part of my life, my daily routine. Sometimes I had nausea. I didn't know when or where I would get dizzy. Once I was at the university, listening to a lecture and started getting dizzy. My lecturer had to ask my classmates to take me to the sick bay.

Another time, I was walking to Isaac's school to pick him up and suddenly felt dizzy. I had to sit down and ask for help. When I got dizzy at work, my colleagues helped me to the staffroom where I would lie on a bed for a few hours. I was getting frustrated day by day as my health was getting worse. I cried and asked God to heal me.

Psalm 130:2 says, *"O Lord, hear my voice. Let your ears be attentive to my cry for mercy."*

The psalmist says, *"I know that the Lord is great, that our Lord is greater than all gods"* (Psalm 135:5).

God reminded me again that He is great, and greater than any problem or sickness. But as a human being, I was disturbed and asked: "God, why did you choose me, why did you give me an autistic child? Now what is happening to my health?" I prayed, "God please show me the way."

My children suffered when I had the dizzy spells. I couldn't give them food or look after them properly. My brother and sister-in-law moved close to my house to look after me. God sent them as angels. I continued to pray and claim His promises. As Psalm 139:14 says,

"I praise you because I am fearfully and wonderfully made, your works are wonderful, I know that full well."

These dizzy spells were ruining my health. Rao took me to an ENT specialist. The doctor asked a few questions and made me do some physical activities, like balancing, which seemed silly. Then he announced the shocking news, "You might have a brain tumour". I was just coming to terms with Mikey's situation, dealing with dizzy spells, nausea and now had to think about a brain tumour. He continued to say, "If you have a brain tumour you should be admitted to the hospital straight away and you'll be operated on, the same day."

Rao looked at my pale face and said, "Don't worry, I know for sure that there's nothing wrong with you. You don't have any brain tumour. God will look after you." I relaxed. The specialist referred me for an MRI scan. I didn't want to wait and instead opted to get the scan done at a private clinic. I quickly got an appointment. I was asked to lie on a mattress and the lady explained to me how she was going to do the scan. I was sent inside a big machine. I quickly closed my eyes and started praying "God please help me, everything has to be normal." Rao was standing beside the machine.

The machine looked scary when I opened my eyes. It was making loud noises, and parts of the machine were moving. I could not watch the machine for long, I had to close my eyes. Thank God my results were normal. There was no brain tumour. I had regular appointments with the ENT doctor at the hospital. But the dizzy spells continued.

Chapter 6

By the time Mikey was 4 years old, he became an extremely fussy eater. He would not eat by himself. He ate Weet-bix for breakfast, bread with Nutella and yoghurt for lunch, and rice and plain yoghurt for dinner.

Toilet-training him was also a problem. In fact, we had to use disposable nappies.

As I began reading up on autism, I discovered new facts every day. Autism/ASD is actually a mental disorder, where a person has a delay or difficulty in communication, social interaction and thinking (cognition). These delays or difficulties are different in each individual. In the case of Mikey, there was a delay in speech. He used to point to objects or take someone's hand to indicate what he wanted. Sometimes he ignored us and we thought he had a hearing problem. But the audiology report said his hearing was normal. Sometimes he repeated what we said, parroting us ('echolalia'). For instance, if I said, "Bye Mikey," he would say "Bye Mikey" as well. Some children with ASD have no speech and some talk freely about specific topics.

Mikey's social interactions were also limited. He did not play with other children. Sometimes he played with Isaac. But Mikey mostly engaged in solitary or observational play with peers. There were occasions when he enjoyed interacting with others and used to push or hit children to provoke reactions and get attention. He didn't respond to other's greetings, smiles or waves. Children with ASD have difficulty in sharing and following social rules. Mikey's thinking (cognition) was also different from other children. Children with ASD do things in a particular way/pattern. Mikey used to line up all his cars. Children over-react to loud noise, and Mikey was very sensitive to loud noise. Mikey had other sensory issues like visual, touch etc. He never participated in messy play or art activities. In fact, he had a strong sensory aversion to certain objects like a peeled banana. He was very active and restless. Mikey likes t-shirts and shorts but always wanted to wear the same clothes. He didn't like new clothes.

Children with ASD find it difficult to cope with changes or new situations. They prefer the same routine and structured programme. They get very upset if there is any change in their routines. Mikey doesn't like surprises and needs to always be aware of what's going on or where he's going. Once, on Mother's day, my husband took us for a surprise lunch. Mikey was not aware of this and wouldn't come out of the car as he was shocked to find out that he was supposed to go for lunch at a restaurant. It took nearly 45 minutes for each family member to try to convince Mikey. In the end, he joined us for the meal. Since then, I've made sure that Mikey knows his schedule beforehand. We tell him where he's going and what he's going to do. He likes routines. He goes to school from Monday to Friday. On Saturdays, we go to Shalom Fellowship, an Indian community group in Auckland. On Sunday, we go to church. Whenever I'm rostered at Sunday school, I prepare Mikey beforehand and display the roster on the fridge which Mikey can access.

We have a big calendar in the kitchen. We write our important appointments on the calendar. Mikey also writes his own appointments and movie dates. Mikey and Isaac together choose movies to watch in the holidays between terms.

Children with ASD have poor coordination or motor skills. I have noticed that Mikey finds it difficult to catch a ball or jump up and down. They have unusual body movements like flapping, spinning, and other repetitive behaviours. For children like Mikey, specialists have developed a different method of education. It's called Individual Educational

Plan (IEP). I found this out at a meeting at Mikey's day care. The educational psychologist, educational support worker, head teacher, centre manager and other professionals who worked with Mikey were at this meeting. They proposed a plan of action for Mikey's educational needs. The plan defined the goals, and the day care provided the resources and support to meet the goals. We then started following the strategies suggested by the team. IEP meetings were held regularly at the daycare to take stock of the progress.

My life was busy with studies, work, dealing with my health issues and attending appointments for Mikey. As the days passed, I informed my parents about the situation at home. As the Christmas holidays were approaching, they asked us to spend a few days with them in India. My parents wanted to take both Mikey and me to the specialist doctors in Hyderabad. We booked our tickets and planned to stay for two months. During the trip I had an appointment with an ENT specialist, who diagnosed my dizzy spells as Vertigo. Vertigo is caused by an inner ear problem. He asked me about my daily routine, and said stress was making me dizzy and I needed some rest. When I started thinking about my routine, I realised I didn't have enough time for rest. I used to do my assignments after the children went to bed. I decided I would change my routine once I returned to Auckland and take more rest.

The doctor prescribed tablets which I had to take when I was dizzy. The tablets made me drowsy and so I took them only for a short while. I couldn't find time to sleep during the day.

A specialist also prescribed medicines for Mikey. Since he was hyperactive, the medicine would help calm him. I explained to my parents about autism. They understood Mikey's situation and supported me by helping with the IEP. I also visited a special needs school in Hyderabad. It was one of the popular schools for special needs children. The children had different special needs. It was also a rehabilitation centre. When I saw the children at the school, I couldn't hold back my tears. There were so many children who needed help. I thanked God for Mikey.

After a good holiday we came back to Auckland. Nothing had really changed in our lives. My dizzy spells were still not under control. I changed my family doctor and the new doctor recommended I go for grommet surgery. She called the hospital and booked an appointment.

A grommet is a tiny plastic tube inserted in the eardrum. The grommet allows air into the space behind the eardrum (middle ear). It's a 15-minute surgery. While I was waiting for my surgery I read Psalm 91 and decided that I would write a poem /song praising God.

By God's grace, I started feeling better and the dizzy spells stopped after the surgery. I thanked God for hearing my cry and healing me. I wrote this poem in His praise. It was taken from Psalm 100.

THANK THE LORD

Let us praise your great and awesome name
Holy is He
Let us exalt the Lord our God
Holy is He
Let us worship His name
Holy is He
Let us worship the Lord who answered my prayers
Holy is He
Let us serve the Lord with gladness
Holy is He

Mikey's second IEP meeting was held at the daycare. This time, the EIT (early intervention teacher) joined the other specialists in the team. After the meeting, the specialists visited our home and showed me how to use visuals with Mikey. Mikey responded well to visuals compared to verbal instructions. I also heard about the Taikura Trust, which supports the differently abled under 65 years of age, and their families and caregivers, in Auckland. The team came to our home and assessed Mikey. They approved 15 days respite care per year. Respite care means caring is provided for the child with special needs, so that the parents can take some time off. They also helped us access timely and appropriate disability support services. The Taikura Trust assesses the needs of the differently abled every three years.

At the daycare, Mikey was in the toddler's room as the team suggested. They thought that once he was settled in the room, they would move him to a pre-school room. Mikey enjoyed singing songs, so the teachers shared their songs and CDs with me. I used to sing with Mikey at home. At church, Mikey used to enjoy the first half of the service as his favourite, the time of worship. He memorised all the songs and his favourite was, "Open the eyes of my heart Lord".

Chapter 7

When Mikey was four, the Picture Exchange Communication System (PECS) was introduced to him. The PECS is used as a communication tool for individuals with ASD. Individuals learn to exchange pictures for items they want. He made great progress and we were all surprised with Mikey's language development. He was taught to use the PECS folder with others and gradually became more confident. It was his means of communication. He approached another person and would give them a picture of the desired item in exchange for that item. Sometimes, he initiated signs "more" and "finished" to communicate. The teaching team also taught me signs which I could use with Mikey.

Every day, Mikey had 30 to 45 minutes of rich stimulating one-to-one teaching with the educational social worker. He was delighted and made significant progress. He recognised letters, numbers, vehicles and words. God has blessed Mikey with a gift of reading and he started reading books at a young age. I took Mikey to a public library and got him a membership. He had his own card which he used to borrow books. Visiting the library became a regular part of our routine. Mikey enjoyed Pokémon, story books, and cartoons, etc.

By the end of 2006, I completed my BA in Early Childhood Education and began working full time at BBCK. I thanked God for helping me throughout my three-year study despite the many hurdles.

Mikey made huge progress. His behaviour was improving. He stopped hitting others. What concerned me was that he was not aware of danger and he still needed to work on his social skills.

We attended regular appointments with the developmental paediatrician with Mikey. At the age of 4 years 5 months, the paediatrician confirmed the ASD diagnosis. Mikey received additional support from the Early Intervention Team from Group Special Education which included a psychologist, speech language therapist, early intervention teacher and educational social worker. This additional support helped Mikey become increasingly sociable with both adults and peers. He engaged in a lot more observational and parallel play and did not attempt to avoid others. He approached adults confidently, sought eye contact and made definite efforts to engage with the person in a manner that he desired.

Mikey used the PECS to construct picture sentences of three to four words. For instance, "I want yellow chicken". He spoke the sentence as he handed the sentence strip over to an adult. He used the PECS at the daycare and at home. I carried Mikey's PECS folder everywhere I took him. But he never uttered a verbal sentence without the picture strip. His literacy has developed alongside the PECS and has an extensive range of basic sight words that he reads. But this did not lead Mikey to general self-initiated speech. He needed the assistance of visuals and routines.

Mikey was going to turn five on the 30th of November 2007. We started looking for a primary school for him. The day care teachers and the GSE team helped us apply for Ongoing and Reviewable Resourcing Schemes (ORRS) funding. ORRS provides (public) funding to support students with high/very high ongoing special education needs at whatever school the student goes to. This funding is available to students throughout their schooling. Mikey has major difficulties with communication and/or social behaviour, but his level of needs did not meet the criteria for ORRS and his funding application was rejected.

Chapter 8

We visited primary schools in our area. Mikey's teaching team suggested the Endeavour Centre, a special needs unit of Mt Roskill Primary School. At the same time, we moved to another suburb. I prepared Mikey for the change by reading a story of moving to another house. Mikey settled very well in the new house. We started contacting schools in our zone. We applied for the ORRS funding a second time, and this time our application was successful and we were able to enrol Mikey at the Endeavour Centre.

In 2008, Mikey started attending full time and was mainstreamed twice a week with an educational support worker. He was part of special needs classroom of 8-10 children, with varying physical, learning and communication needs. As Mikey still had a restricted diet, the teachers introduced one new food a week. He had very poor chewing habits and would often swallow things whole. He didn't close his mouth properly and would spill while drinking. His behaviour became unpredictable but he wasn't aggressive towards other children. He started screaming and occasionally pushed others.

At school, Mikey received regular support from the centre occupational therapist, speech language therapist, and physiotherapist. He attended ESOL (English for Speakers of Other Languages) classes three times each week. Gradually, he became more flexible within the school programme and was willing to take part in new activities. We focused on making him more independent. The Ministry of Education (MOE) funds specialised equipment and modifications, like laptops, for children like Mikey. He was very good with the iPad and laptop. He mastered them quickly and enjoyed using internet resources, playing games and watching YouTube videos and commentaries.

The SLT discussed with us the possibility of trying a communication device (talking computer) with Mikey. He was waiting for the Talklink Trust to complete an assessment of his communication needs. In the meanwhile, the SLT used Dynavox Maestro with Mikey. Mikey liked Dynavox, and I was shown how to use it with him. Dynavox helps people to communicate, as well as aiding their language and literacy development. I shared Mikey's favourite things with the SLT so she could upload them to the communication device. These included SpongeBob, Tom and Jerry, McDonalds, football, cricket, hockey, golf etc.

Mikey's pencil grip (five finger grip) was awkward, which impacted his writing ability. He used Toontastic and Puppet Pals to make up little plays, and Book Creator and Strip Designer apps on the iPad. He enjoyed typing his work into PowerPoint or Word and used photos of activities at school. Sometimes he downloaded pictures from the internet to support his writing. He could write simple sentences, usually about his personal experiences. He used the iPad with the TouchChat communication app to support his social activities and for language development. He used learned phrases and sentences to engage with others which were sometimes not relevant to the situation. He could follow simple instructions and a daily routine.

Mikey was friendly, caring and loving. He liked to hug and kiss people including strangers. The teaching team helped me write a social story about hugging and kissing family members, but not strangers. I read the story frequently to Mikey. We continued to coach and model appropriate social language and social behaviours with him.

Going to the toilet was still a concern. He often didn't go until it was urgent. He also needed constant prompts to check and clean the toilet after he used it.

I always wanted to find out more about autism, including what it was and why it happened, and in 2012, I successfully completed a Postgraduate Certificate in Specialist Teaching in Autism from Massey University.

Chapter 9

Mikey went through several phases of pushing, screaming, swearing etc. Each phase continued for nearly six months. It was very tough for us to cope with these phases. I was frustrated and sometimes shouted at Mikey to stop screaming or swearing. I was embarrassed when Mikey was going through these phases, especially when we were shopping or when we were at church. People who didn't know what was happening would stare at us instead of helping. I slowly got used to this and learned not to care what others thought about me or my child. Social stories help children with autism to better understand communication and social skills. I used social stories for most of the phases he was going through, which helped Mikey to come out of them.

Mikey is currently in a self-talking phase. He talks to himself most of the time. Sometimes he just repeats cartoons or commentaries he has watched. We are reminding Mikey about when it is an appropriate time to talk, especially in the classroom.

Mikey's love for technology has been evident since he was a child. He used the desktop and laptop, and was competent with log-in procedures. He could plug in a USB mouse, power lead and headphones in the correct ports and also had good keyboard skills. He understood the relevant drives on the school's network to manage his files and folders. He could load a CD into the CD-ROM drive. He was also able to complete activities on Mouse Skills and use the Jig Saw Maker programme to assemble puzzles. He used Mega Mix to complete dot to dot drawings, and computer skills programmes to complete puzzles and eye tracking games. He enjoyed early learning software like Tizzy's Toybox, ABC Talking Alphabet, and Reader Rabbit Preschool.

For the first time, Mikey attended school camps in years five and six. He had never stayed away from the family before. I wrote a social story about school camp which I read to Mikey frequently, preparing him for the camp. It was a new, challenging experience, which he enjoyed and actively participated in.

Mikey has participated in a school production where he played the role of a chicken. He performed all five days in the evenings after school. He was given a choice to perform only three days. He enjoyed performing on stage. I was surprised to see Mikey on stage with a group of other children. He waited patiently for his part and was on stage for 30 minutes.

Mikey usually needed reminders to greet family members for birthdays or special occasions. When he was eight, on my birthday, he said, "Happy Birthday Mummy," without anyone prompting him.

By then, Mikey had nearly finished primary school and was getting ready to go to intermediate school. As per the suggestions of the teaching team, we enrolled Mikey at the Tennyson Centre, a special needs unit of Mt Roskill Intermediate School. As part of the transition process, he was introduced to his new teacher aide, teacher, and classroom. He regularly visited his classroom. The following year Mikey joined the Tennyson Centre. He settled well in the new classroom and made new friends. He was invited for birthday parties which he thoroughly enjoyed. We always attended school picnics and Christmas parties.

Mikey doesn't like sleepovers at other places. Once or twice he has stayed with my nieces but otherwise he likes to sleep at home. He also likes to be on the stage. He shared his testimony at the Blockhouse Bay Community Church. He sings songs and shares his stories with others at the Shalom Fellowship. In the end he even asks the audience to clap for him.

Mikey is nearly 14 years old now. He enjoys making PowerPoints, making commentaries, commenting on others' commentaries on YouTube, movies on Toontastic etc. He loves to dance and sings the latest songs. Reading is still his favourite. We frequently visit our local library.

Next year, Mikey will be going to high school. He was accepted at MacLean Centre, Mt Roskill Grammar School. As part of the interview, he had to interact with the manager of the centre for 15 minutes. He did well.

I always wonder how God works in our lives and His works are marvellous. God is faithful and always fulfils His promises in our lives. I am not sure what would have happened if Mikey was born in India. The support and resources which he is getting here might not be available in India. I believe that it was God's plan for us to move to New Zealand. I thank God for all the things He has done in my life. God has a plan and purpose in my life and Mikey's life as well. I am not worried about Mikey's future as God is in control of everything. Mikey has made great progress and improved a lot. He enjoys singing gospel songs, reads the Bible, and prays every day. God will definitely use Mikey mightily to extend His kingdom. I believe that God is with me, and that His angels are watching over me and my family.

Michael's poem

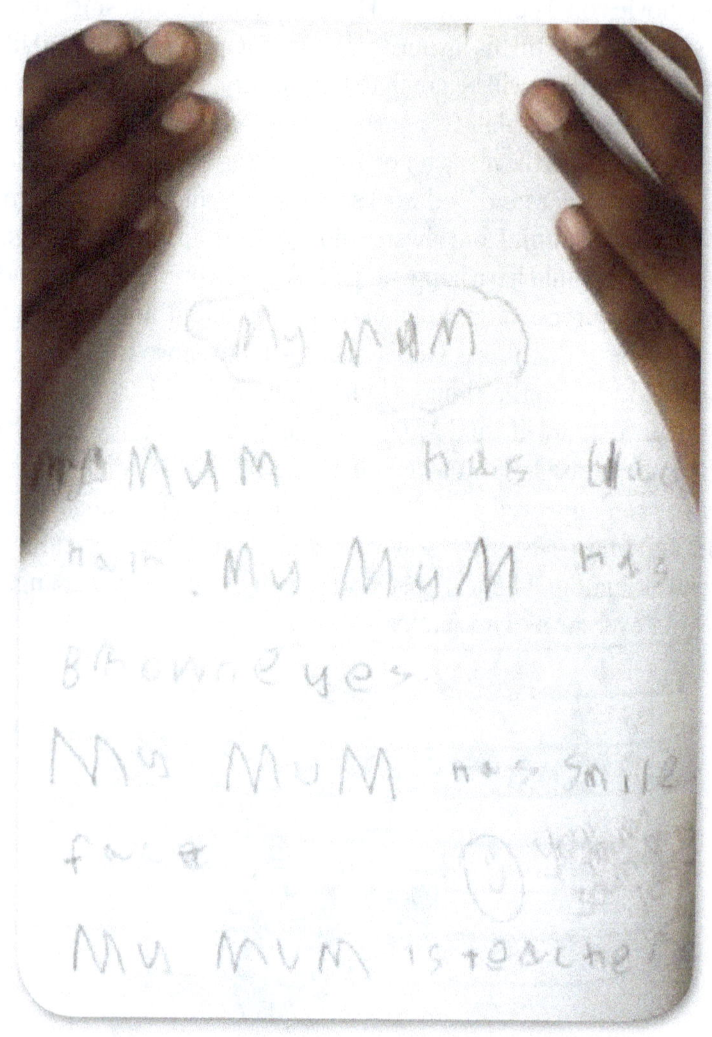

Poems I have appreciated during difficult times

BASED ON PSALM 103

Bless the Lord O my soul
Bless His Holy name
Who forgives all our iniquity
Who heals all our diseases
Who redeems our life from the pit
Who crowns us with steadfast love and mercy
Who satisfies us with good
Who is righteous and justice
Who is merciful and gracious
Who is slow to anger and abounding in steadfast love
Who shows compassion to those who fear him
Who has established his throne in the heavens
Bless the Lord O my soul
Bless His Holy name

PRAISE AND WORSHIP

I will sing of your love, O Lord
I will walk with you, O Lord
I will ponder on you, O Lord
I will proclaim your word, O Lord
I will give thanks to you, O Lord
I will praise you, O Lord
I will tell of all your wonders, O Lord
I will be glad and rejoice in you, O Lord
I will praise the Lord, who counsels me, O Lord
I will sing praise to your name, O Lord
I will declare your name to all, O Lord
I will dwell in the house forever, O Lord
I will exalt you, O Lord

I will give you thanks, O Lord
I will praise you forever for what you have done, O Lord
I will praise you in the presence of your saints, O Lord
I will praise as long as I live, O Lord
I will lift up my hands in your name, O Lord
I will shout with Joy to you, O Lord
I will glorify with thanksgiving, O Lord
I will proclaim your righteousness, O Lord
I will praise you more and more, O Lord
I will remember the deeds of you, O Lord
I will remember your miracles, O Lord
I will meditate on all your works, O Lord
I will consider all your mighty deeds, O Lord
I will listen to what you will say, O Lord
I will sing of your great love forever, O Lord
I will establish your line forever, O Lord
I will make your throne firm through all generations, O Lord
I will maintain my love forever, O Lord

BASED ON PSALM 67-68

May God
May God be gracious
May God make his face shine on us
May God show his ways to us
May God rule us with equity
May God guide us on the earth
May God bless us
May God make the righteous be glad
May God give abundant showers
May God offer inheritance
May God provide for the poor
May God dwell

Samples of social stories

SAYING "HELLO"

I say "hello" to Mum.
I say "hello" to Dad.
I say "hello" to Isaac.
I give them a hug.
At school I say "hello" to my friends and I wave my hand.
I say "hello" to my teachers.
I wave my hand.
If I am sad or hurt, teachers may give me a hug.
When I meet people I don't know,
I can say "hello" and wave my hand.
Well done, Michael.

THE END

Sleeping in my bed

Sometimes Mum, Dad, Isaac and I might stay at a camp,
a motel, or with friends for the night.
Most nights I sleep at home.

After dinner I get ready for bed.
I brush my teeth and put on my pyjamas.
I get into bed.

Mum or Dad might:
- Read me a story
- Make up a story with me
- Let me read a book quietly.

When we go to sleep it is usually night time and dark outside.
Mum or Dad turn off my bedroom light.

I can think about things I like when I am in bed
- Riding my bike
- Playing cricket
- My favourite books

Sleeping at night time is important so that our bodies can rest and grow.
It is good to sleep or to rest in my bed at night time.

Waking Up At Night Time

Sometimes I wake up in the night time when it is dark.

I stay in my bed and rest my body.
I might feel scared or worried and want to go to Mum and Dad.
I can stay in my bed and think about things I like:
- Riding my bike
- Playing cricket
- My favourite books

Mum and Dad are in their bed.
Isaac is in his bed.
I stay in my bed and think about things I like.
Mum, Dad and Isaac need to sleep at night too.

When it is morning my family wake up.
I know it is morning because the sun is up and it is light now.
I might hear Mum or Dad getting up.
We get out of bed.
It is time for breakfast and to get ready for a new day.
I am learning to stay in my bed and rest at night time.
Mum and Dad are happy when I stay in my bed and rest.

THE END

We are moving to a new house

We can pack all our things in boxes.
We can write our names on the boxes so we know who they belong to.
We can write on the boxes what is inside them too.

Our new address is 9b, Riversdale Road, Avondale.
A big truck and some strong men will take our furniture
to our new house.

Moving to a new house is an exciting adventure.
Sometimes I might miss my old house.
When that happens I can look at pictures of the old house,
or tell a story I remember about the old house,
or draw a picture of my old house.

I am moving to a new house with my family on 19th April 2014.
The new house will not look the same as the house that I live in now.
The new house will have 3 bedrooms, a kitchen, a living room
and a bathroom.
They might look different and they might feel different.
That's okay with me.
I loved my old house but I will try to love my new house too.
That will make my family happy.
That will make me happy too.

THE END

My holiday in India

We are going on a special family holiday to Hyderabad in India on the 30th of November 2013. Hyderabad is a warm place with lots of people and traffic. I will hear people speaking the Telugu language in Hyderabad.

Before we go, we need to pack our suitcase. My parents can help me with this. Here are some things that we will take:

- T-shirts
- Shorts/pants
- Tooth brush, soap, towel
- PS Vita, iPod, book

I am lucky because I get to celebrate my 11th birthday in the plane. I am going with my daddy and Isaac. Mummy will join us after 2 weeks. We will drive to Auckland airport and then get on a Singapore plane to fly to Singapore. The flight will take 8 hours.

During the flight, I can:
- Watch movies and cartoons
- Listen to music
- Read a book
- Have some rest
- Eat meals

When we arrive in Singapore, we will stay in a hotel; we will have dinner and sleep the night there. In the morning we will get on a plane to Hyderabad. This flight will take 3½ hours. During the flight, I can listen to music or read a book.

When we arrive in Hyderabad, we will meet Ammamma (nana) and other people in the airport. We will drive to Ammamma's house - this will take about 1 hour. We will have our own bedroom. I will stay in my bed all night. We will also stay with Atha (aunty) & Mama (uncle) for some time.

Mummy will join us on the 14th of December 2013. We all go to the airport to get mummy. We will go to daddy's village by train. We will stay there for 2 days.

We will go back to Hyderabad by train. We will celebrate Christmas and New Year with our family members.

Things we might like to do in Hyderabad:

- Visit some of our relatives
- Attend a wedding ceremony
- Go to church
- Visit the Museum and Zoo
- Do some shopping
- Travel by train or bus or auto-rickshaw
- Visit the Taj Mahal

We will all come back together to Auckland on the
14th of January 2014, after one month in India.

I am excited about going on holiday and I will enjoy my holiday.

THE END

My jobs

clean
fold clothes
trash bags
sweep
wash windows
dust
clean bathroom
wipe table
water plants
letter box
empty trash
take out trash
rake

My jobs – To Do List

	What have I to do	Tick off when task is done ☑
Task 1		
Task 2		
Task 3		

3 ticks =

When I am finished I choose what I do.